33 Years of Untold Secrets

There's a bit of Secret in All of Us

Maisoon Al Saleh

33 Years of Untold Secrets

MAISOON AL SALEH

33 Years of Untold Secrets – There's a bit of Secret in All of Us
Copyright ©2021 by Maisoon Al Saleh
All rights reserved. No portion of this book may be reproduced, stored in whole or part in a retrieval system, or transmitted in any form or by any means including graphic, electronic, mechanical, photocopy, recoding, or any other means except in the case of brief quotations embodied in critical articles and oral reviews, without the prior written consent of the publisher. Reasonable efforts were made to trace the copyright holders and if there are any errors or requirements for adjustments, contact us on the addresses below. In addition, we would be pleased to add appropriate acknowledgements in later prints/editions.

Paperback ISBN: 978-1-7378373-2-9
Digital online Ebook ISBN: 978-1-7378373-3-6

PO box 236210, Dubai, UAE
Website: www.maisoonalsaleh.com
Email: info@thepaintlystore.com

33 Years of Untold Secrets

I would like to dedicate this book to my mother who is the foundation of my well being and success.

Through this book, I wish my readers extract motivation and inspiration to never give up.

Hold on, you'll get there.

Table of Contents

CHAPTER ONE 1

CHAPTER TWO 15

CHAPTER THREE 35

CHAPTER FOUR 56

CHAPTER FIVE 81

CHAPTER SIX 97

Chapter One

Seed of the Soul

"We provide ourselves enough to grow, but we often leave our soul behind."

Often at night, you count the things you own, and the people you have only to end up questioning what is missing. The calculation doesn't seem to fit, it stresses you out, and the only solution you find at that moment is to sleep through it. However, regardless of how many nights you skip through sleep, the reality is eventually going to confront you, in ways you might not have comprehended.

It is said, life isn't fair. Conversely, to be a bit realistic, are we fair to ourselves? We grow, and we groom only to survive, let alone live. Soon, our soul begins to starve. We starve ourselves of the very rudiments our soul is reliant upon.

Amidst a busy day, quite similar to every other day we've spent, we break down. We exhaust ourselves and look around finding origins to hold accountable. While all that time, it was within.

Your passion is what keeps your soul alive; the element that helps you strive for better.

I, Maisoon Al Saleh, was born in 1988 in Dubai. I do not quite remember how life was for me in the beginning, but as my mother narrates it, it was indeed a blessed one. Soon after my birth, my parents travelled to Seattle, United States of America, as my father was studying English Language.

My first steps were in Seattle, where life is as busy as a cat in a hot tin roof. The first word that came out of my mouth was *Abu,* when I was trying to say father in Arabic. My father suggested the name Maisoon at the time of my birth, and my mother happily agreed to it. I was close to my mother. Not only did she provide me a life worth remembering, but she cherished me as a blessing, and supported me in places I could not have survived alone. I am grateful for the sacrifices she made in order to raise me. I believe nothing I do can ever compare to that. My mother couldn't complete her university studies as she was completely occupied with me. She married to her cousin at an early age. Hence, she didn't really have a choice when

I was born.

Mothers are the only beings who know how to give, and do not wish to take anything in return.

Childhood is the most fragile part of our lives, it can mold us into someone we ought to be, or into someone, we might regret someday. My mother was careful with my emotions, my life, and me. She ensured I was raised the way I deserved and stood by me in every walk of life.

My first birthday was celebrated in Seattle as well. However, soon we migrated to Michigan as my father was then pursuing his master's degree.

Like every child of my age, I wasn't aware of what life had in store for me. I was gradually growing into a keen observer with a curious mind. I went to Kindergarten in Michigan, and life was just as it was supposed to be.

If you look around and see a world full of life, it's because there's life inside you.

I soon made friends in the neighborhood, one of which I still remember: Terry. We used to play around and bake cookies together. I was only two but had a strong hold on grasping knowledge and implementing it on my life. However, this did not change the fact that I was just a child, and I too, walked towards troubles myself.

My mother's memory is ironically vivid. It is as if we lived it yesterday. She often talks about the time she came to pick me up from Terry's place, and I was covered in white flour.

I usually stare at my mother's eyes when she reminisces the times of my adolescence. I see how her eyes light up, silently wishing to live those moments again.

Maybe that is how mothers are, pure and full of love.

With life increasing inside of her, she once narrated another event of when I was a child.

My friend Terry knocked at my door once and told my mother I had peed on the stairway. Humorously, this did instill a wave of embarrassment upon my mother and she quickly turned to me and asked for answers. I too, was a bit mortified and apologized as my mother asked me to.

I was always the kind to analyze the severity of the situation and act accordingly.

However, this did not change the fact that I was quite a trouble maker, and I was often caught having fun to an extent that was the center of everyone's attention. I wasn't a child who was sensitive, I did feel but never enough to cry easily. I was usually found dancing in class along with my classmates.

The most cherished element in how my parents raised me is the fact that they shaped my decision making. They ensured I was given room to choose and decide for myself, which led me to a life where I am able to think critically before moving further. I was never waived off my rights. In fact, I was reminded of it often.

As a child, I chose what to wear in Halloween. I remember being a fairy, a turtle, and a lion. However, gradually my lively soul and curious mind led to something that identified my talent and fueled my passion.

It all started when I picked up a crayon and began scribbling…

What's inside you, will eventually come out.

Just like any mother would, my mother observed my actions quite closely. She noticed me coloring without any complications. To her, and anyone for that matter, was a shock. A child with the perfect sense to not scribble outside the lines was indeed an achievement.

She instantly knew this was special, and that I had a gift inside me waiting to be acknowledged.

I wasn't at all the delicate kind, was brave enough to love insects and snakes. In fact, according to my mother, I used to catch them with my bare hands.

We moved to Dubai after four years and began my schooling from a provide institution. My Arabic wasn't good enough to be in a government school hence a private school wasn't really a choice. However, my intelligence at such an age rewarded me with a skipped grade. I could tell how proud my mother was. Being born in Seattle, my accent was a bit American, enough to confuse my mother at times as to what was I trying to say. This was when my father stepped in to be the translator and fill in the communication gap. My mind was sharp because of my mother. She engaged me in mind games since my childhood and it only groomed my thought process.

Her parenting and decisions stabled my mind enough to take

responsibility since a young age. My younger sisters became my responsibility and I looked after them willingly.

However, these weren't the only reasons that placed me in the limelight. I had a noticeable element in my appearance which often led to an uncomfortable position. My back was curved, and somehow, everyone had an opinion about it.

I was often criticized over it, enough to question my own worth. I clearly didn't accept who I was completely, and every opinion had an effect on me. I remember someone suggested I should wear a metallic back support belt, and it ended up bruising my body. However, I grew and eventually accepted myself in its entirety, and I vow to never fall back again.

You are exactly how you're supposed to be.

This world needs quite a therapy, we've all been in places where we were the victim, or the perpetrator, and be it the slightest of negativity. For a long time I was consumed with thoughts of how I should mend who I am, and become what everybody is. It not only compromised my self-worth, it decreased my confidence as well. However, I am glad I know better. I mean, maybe this is the curve I've got. Nonetheless, I am grateful for who I am and I couldn't have asked to be anyone else, or any different.

When I was born, the size of my head was unusual. My mother recalls she had to place pillows on the side just to hold my head up while she made me sit.

Mothers are like that, loving unconditionally, never minding what compromises they make, or uneasy situations they cater just to be with us, and keep us safe. It's amazing you know, the fact that you have someone who loves you to the moon and never back, someone who looks at all your flaws and doesn't feel you have any.

A mother's love, is indeed a blessing.

Love isn't always about a romantic relationship, it comes in forms quite different, and unusual as well. For me, when I look in the mirror and feel content and accepted by myself, that's pure love.

Love for me is when my mother reminds me of how I used to be, the times when I was young enough to not jot down those memories myself.

Love is when my mother knew I had a gift even before me. Love for me is when I pick up the brush, and paint out my heart and mind. Love for me is to pursue my dreams further. Love is all around, in places we mostly miss and do not pay attention too.

Love, my friend, is enough.

They say, artists pour out their pain through utensils on canvases. I, however, pour out my happiness. Each time I feel happy, I choose to let out the artist in me and create a masterpiece, and the end result is always an achievement. Nonetheless, I am human, and to feel happy is a moment that comes in waves. Hence, the limited paintings I have compared to other mediums like digital art.

Chapter Two

The Skeleton Blooms

"Time is a concept made by man, it has no rules, it might slow down for one, while flow hastily for the other. However, there's one thing constant: It keeps moving."

Growing up you wonder what life ahead would be like, and when you finally reach there, all you do is look back and reminisce.

I wasn't really a quiet child, trouble was always around me. I was always caught engaged in some fun or mischievous act. However, they were harmless.

When I was in grade 2 or 3, I remember I was given a separate room, however, locking it up wasn't even up for consideration. I pretty much gave those reasons though.

In fact, my door didn't even have keys. This was so my parents could keep a close eye on me (for all the right reasons).

I had given them many but I was sure that one moment was the last straw. My mom opened my drawer and found a dead rat inside my pencil case! I don't really remember why I chose to do that, but all I know for sure is that moment had gotten me famous, and I was soon known as the girl with a dead rat in her pencil case!

Moments do not define you, but people remember, recognize and build your presence in their mind through it.

When I think of it, I believe I gave my parents a hard time when I was a child. They were anxious because of my mischievousness, and all I wanted was a little time for myself. However, this was only possible if I hid under my bed, with my papers and colors. It was incredibly calming and quiet. Not for long though, I had to be careful because my parents often came in searching for me, and I'm glad I wasn't spotted.

Growing up was fun, but now when I look back, nostalgia creeps in quite overwhelmingly, making me realize a huge part of me I have left behind, although I still am mischievous, times back then were rare.

When I was in grade 4, I began participating in dance battles. My demeanor was that of someone tiny but fierce. I was into pop music and the victory was always mine.

This was the time when I began investing more into art. I sold my first artworks at the age of 13 or 14 in a school art exhibition. Each of them were sold for an average of $13 to $28. My energy was flourishing and I began freelancing on the side. I have always had the mindset of having my own finances. Being independent was really something I believe in since I was a child.

Moreover, my mind always came up with distinctive ideas. For instance, it was Eid, a Muslim occasion, and there's a tradition where elders distribute money to the youngsters. I used to auction my old stuff to them.

It was business for me, however, a shock to my mother when she noticed all my sister's money was missing.

You only fear what you haven't witnessed.

My life was filled with moments of happiness and sadness, each of which helped me learn, and gain knowledge. I had a habit of extracting something from everything that passed me by, and my parents enrolling me into a summer program during my school break was just one of them.

It was a summer program to learn swimming, ice skating and bowling. And while the latter two seemed easier, the former was a bit scary. I stood at the end of the pool at the deep end's side, staring at the water gradually making its wavy texture, I was nowhere near to what could happen to me next.

Splash! And I went into the pool as my swimming trainer pushed me. However, I rose to the surface and understood what had happened. It was a lesson, and a lesson I had learnt quite well. If the decision was left on me, I might have decided to not face my fears, and since I had, I now knew there was nothing to fear about. And as soon as the realization struck, I ended up competing in my school's swimming contest, and receiving a medallion. In addition,

I was awarded a trophy in a hula-hoop contest as well!

You only discover your true potential when you've left with no choice.

I didn't have much friends in high school, but the time I spent there is a collection of wonderful memories I hold dear.

My seat was always different from the others, it was zebra. It was a black and white stripped chair with wheels, which twisted from the sides while I tried my best to concentrate on my studies during class. The chair was comfortable though, I could relax the entire time while studying. It was delivered specifically for me. I could tell I wasn't the only one liking it as kids around often stared at it with excitement. I came to know later they played with it in my absence or during my sick leaves.

My school days were one of a kind, most of them were moments I remember clearly, as I was at an age to hold memories.

My back's posture was a bit curved as compared to others, this often became a point of discussion for those around me. Somehow, people always felt the need to either give me advices on how to correct it, or worse: make fun of it. I was severely criticized and it made me often think I must do something about it.

Honestly, it affected me. When people looked at me and noticed it, instead of several other aspects of mine which I could be proud of, it affected me within. I remember being influenced enough to listen to advices of wearing a metallic belt which in turn bruised my stomach and I ended up bleeding at times because I was given one not customized to my size. It took me a long while to realize a curved back does not define me, and I was more than what I looked like, and I definitely had more to offer than just my appearance. I had brains, and I had a knack for talents quite rare, and as soon as I gained a grip on myself, I wore confidence quite easily and accepted myself openly and proudly.

You were meant to be this way. You're unique, and that's the gift. Embrace it.

People will never love you for who you are, unless you begin to love yourself wholeheartedly first. It is you, upon which it depends. Else the world has a lot of hate to offer anyways.

High school is a time when children are on the verge of maturing, and their brains are most efficient in adapting the surroundings, and extracting information. I was, indeed, the same.

I remember vividly how sharp and naughty I was, and as a trouble maker, it was certainly my duty to produce a mess every once a while.

Hence, it was summer time, and it was extremely hot. I along with my classmates decided to fill up balloons with water and play around to beat the heat. It was merely a solution for the summer, and what worse could possibly happen?

Well… Little I knew I was inviting trouble – yet again!

While we were fighting by bursting the balloons on each other during break, the bell rang and it was time for the fun to be over. However, I believe we were a bit too invested at that moment, and instead of wrapping up the game, the balloon accidentally slipped from my hand. No, this was certainly not the problem, the problem was where it actually slipped and fell.

Yes. As I gazed above and saw, I realized I hadn't just invited trouble, I had invited my worst nightmare.

Of all the people in my high school, the balloon had slipped and fallen onto our school principal!

The minute I saw her all wet and soaked, I panicked and crawled down. I had to come up with an explanation, but what could it be?

Possibly saving her from a heat stroke? I had no explanation, and every excuse I came up with me knew was a dead end.

Therefore, I ran to the toilet, closed the door and purposely didn't lock it.

I knew she would come around searching for the culprit so I didn't want her to believe someone was inside hiding. I even stood on top of the toilet seat with my head tucked in like a rolled hedgehog, in hopes I wouldn't get caught.

I was trying not to breathe heavily, even though my anxiousness was taking a toll on me.

It was if I was in a movie scene, trying to either escape a monster of a possible killer.

Amidst of me praying to get out of the mess I created, I heard footsteps closing in.

I could feel it was my ill-fate closing in, searching for me.

Thankfully, I heard she left without realizing I was inside, and finally, I breathed a sigh of relief.

Phew, it was a close call.

It is all fun and games until you get caught.

I was growing up and my 16th birthday came. I must say, I was gifted the most thoughtful gift ever by my father.

It was an art studio, and he got it custom made carefully, knowing how I would like it the best. He built it right beside our house in the garden; a beautiful cube-like structure colored white, with one side of the whole wall as a window from the bottom till the ceiling.

At that moment, I just looked at it as the most amazing gift. However, what I wasn't aware of was the magic it possessed, for that very art studio became home to where all my dreams grew, progressed, and came to life.

You look at what's ahead of you, and you appreciate it for existing. However, you will never be aware of how much of a blessing something is until you one day look back and see the progress.

Ah, Nemo was his name, the dearest to me. I still remember it as if it were yesterday. Truly beautiful. His hazel eyes were breathtaking, and definitely the kind to get lost into. I remember just staring at Nemo for minutes. I know, I was creepy.

By now, you might be wondering what sort of a dog or cat was Nemo. Well, Nemo was my pet snake!

Nemo meant the world to me, it used to wander around my bedroom, and often slept beside me on my bed. I loved him dearly.

Honestly, there were times I sneaked him into the school inside my bag pack, and we attended classes together.

I was quite a mischief to be honest. Looking at it now, I just want to say… I have no regrets. Those were probably the only things that helped me believe in life, stay energetic and increased my desire to grow.

This reminds me of the day my mother called me in anger, boy, she was furious.

"Maisoon! You will give me a heart attack someday!"

I wasn't really sure of what I had done, probably because I had done a lot of things. I kept quiet. I knew my mother was on a volcano mode, and anything wrong might just erupt her. I stayed calm and said, "Is everything okay, mother?"

"Okay? Okay??? I nearly died! I opened your art studio and saw a big skeleton staring right at my face!"

As much as I wanted to calm her down, I couldn't help being myself. I burst into laughter and said, "Oh, he was just guarding my studio!" The skeleton was a friend in there. He had seen me groom my skills, and I used to dress it up at times. I remember taking funny pictures with it... This wasn't it, I used to dance with it as well, but I wish I could do more. It was quite heavy to carry around. However, my nature didn't allow me to not even give it a try.

It was a waste, though. I remember it splitting into two. It was funnier to see the head rolling everywhere, and the body in my arms. However, the fun didn't last long, as I had to put it back together.

Meanwhile, I had started painting and selling my art around in my institution as well. I wanted to test the products of my founded company before I formally launched it. My sister, Khulood, was the only person who made me laugh and entertained me the most. She often helped me in selling my products as well. Back then, I used to stand on the stalls and sell my products myself. People didn't know I was the owner of the entire business, to them I was a seller. In fact, they thought I was working for a company.

However, soon enough, my business began to expand, and I hosted my products at a huge annual carnival. As I began profiting, I hired more people to stand at the stall. This business of manufacturing handmade T-shirts etc. soon was in demand and I was shipping my products. I always had this in mind, to be able to profit from my skill. My mind was driven and energetic, I always had ideas I could implement on, and carry forward.

However, there were times I embarrassed myself. Enough, to question my being, really.

I accidentally drank the water cup I had been cleaning my brushes with instead of my cup of juice. I guess when they say art comes from within, I truly believed it!

I really have no idea where I was lost, or what I was thinking. It was probably something artistic or mischievous in my mind, though it backfired.

The minute the taste of paint went down my throat, I ran towards the toilet to puke it out. I couldn't though.

What you find negative, or only memories and lessons in the making.

Everything wasn't really all fun and games. I remember my friends calling me and telling me they had been accepted by several universities and had their options to ponder over. I, on the other hand, got accepted by one university, and it didn't quite have the exact studies I had planned on pursuing. It was a government university, Zayed University and the closest to my desired major, architecture, was Interior Design, hence I enrolled right away. I wasn't efficient in Arabic and as this was a government university I had to make sure I was. So I made extra efforts as compared to the Emirati Students and took Arabic classes after school.

While I thought I had enrolled in studies I didn't quite wanted, I didn't know it would turn out to be exactly what I needed.

What you desire may just not be what you need to grow!

Interior Design, in fact, helped me convert 2D art into 3D perspective, I remember making my whole room into a canvas. I remember it all began with a simple small flat surface, and gradually my entire room was my canvas!

From there I could see what I was learning could actually take me a long way, and boy, I never stopped since.

I gradually began creating sculptures, installations, and interactive art.

While in the beginning I thought I didn't really have a choice, what I wasn't aware of was how this would turn out to be the best career decision I had really made!

I learned so much during that time, my skills were not only polishing and grooming, in fact, they were broadening. I was truly a proud Zayed University Graduate.

Life really was blossoming and going how I had once dreamt of. In fact, it was even better.

Soon my tenure at Zayed University was over and I had graduated. I took a sigh of relief and looked at what I had achieved so far.

Although my achievements weren't so huge, I knew how hard I had worked for it.

I graduated from the university with a GPA of 2.49 which fell in between B- which was considered as a 2.7 and C+ which was considered 2.3.

I was grateful for it, the beginning was a bit distorted as I was given an academic warning because of getting an F in Global Studies I.

However, after the first semester everything began to fall into place, although, I still had a D in Arabic Concepts. Nonetheless, I worked efficiently and aced a B in Arabic Lab later.

While my grades were a bit shaky in these subjects, I was acing straight A's in world cultures in art and design, art foundation, color and light design, independent studies, and the professional artist.

Through experience I have learned, and strongly believe that grades are just numbers, and true achievement is in what information and grooming have we extracted from it.

I was excited, the time to learn and groom was technically over, and I was now out in the world to implement it.

I had plans, and I had dreams, and I certainly wasn't someone to let them go.

However, what is life really, I realized I had stepped into a part which wasn't as rainbows and butterflies as the previous one.

The level had upgraded, and I wasn't really prepared of what practical life had in store for me.

For starters, my art studio became too small for me to work comfortably. To be able to concentrate on my work, I required a peaceful environment. I've been renting for the last six years and a few months of my life, but I've just purchased my first home finally. I needed a small apartment with enough room for my paints, canvases, and paintings to be hung on the walls, as well as a kitchen where I could make chocolate brownies. A robot named Num Num also came to live with me... He got his name from the fact that he eats dust and the little cactuses on my balcony, which I water on occasion.

You wouldn't really know until you walk through it yourself, alone.

Chapter Three

The Bones Grew

"Life isn't a dead beat, to stay still all along. It beats from constant ups and downs, and that is exactly what life is all about."

I wasn't sure of how smooth my life would go in the near future. However all I knew was I wasn't going to stop anywhere, my energy was full, and I had no intentions of taking my life slow.

All was going fine until the time of my ultra lazik operation came near. The more essential I was told it was, the more I got scared.

I was an artist after all, and my imagination clearly had no boundaries. While this may be a blessing, it sometimes becomes a curse in anxious situations.

At the time of my ultra lazik operation, I was petrified. I could even smell my eyes burning. The only thoughts lingering in my mind were whether I'll be able to see again.

Luckily, my eyesight is better even now than what it used to be. However, it did drop back a little after ten years of doing it.

Nonetheless, with it came several struggles but I did not back down. I remember once I gave a speech on stage about my artistic path as part of a well-known speaking event. There was a slight tremor in my voice at the beginning of my speech because I had the ultra-lasik eye surgery the day before and was supposed to be resting at home in a dark room. The organizers agreed with me to turn off the stage spotlight that was shining directly into my eyes so that I wouldn't be distracted while I spoke because of the irritation. However, after I entered the stage, they switched it on for some unknown reason. During that speech, the anguish was unbearable, and to this day, it is unforgettable.

My activities and interests only grew with time, and soon I found myself interested in scuba diving, on top of it, I was learning to paint underwater.

It was just another lesson, and it was supposed to end the same way but life had a little twist written for me, and soon I came to know of what it was.

As I was descending the water, I realized I had begun to choke. The water had burst all of a sudden into my mouth, and I was instantly losing breath. At that moment, I had no other thought than the one continuously telling me I was going to die.

I could feel it was the end, and all that mattered at that moment was to be given a chance at life again. My hope was fading in minutes until my buddy diver grabbed my fin to ensure I did not damage my lungs. I was gradually losing conscious until I finally did. The last thing I remember was my jacket was inflated and I was coughing for a breath of air.

Thankfully, I was saved and I couldn't believe I was breathing again.

I had been given life again, and that was the most appreciative moment of my life.

Learning to paint underwater was definitely not a walk in the park. Nonetheless, I never backed down.

I enjoy fishing, but after several attempts, I've never been able to land a fish. I've only ever caught and released one fish in my life, a pufferfish.

Going back to the time when my father named me Maisoon, he clearly gave a lot of thought to it.

Till today, people often misspell my name. It used to bother me before, but now I enjoy the experience. Moreover, they even referred to me as Mr Maisoon in hotels, restaurant bookings, and other correspondences.

It used to set me off really. I am even called Maison at times, which is a house in French. I came across people who actually believed I owned every single property that had Maison written on it.

I prefer not to sign contracts have my name misspelled, that too, the first time. The very thought of working with a company which wouldn't get my name right didn't make me comfortable. Coming to the point where I actually enjoyed these hilarious moments was when people were pacing back and forth to find Mr Maisoon while I sipped my coffee observing them calmly in plain sight. This happened during my own private company trips.

My career of visual art, mainly of skeletons began with my diptych, an acrylic painting called, "Until Death Do Us Apart." The art reflects a male and female skeleton who're wearing a traditional wedding attire. The concept was based on a real couple who passed away.

Diptych is a form of art which consists of two panels, or two parts; such was the case with my art piece. Before I knew it, it became the center of attention for everyone who saw it.

My art is never the one to just soothe the eyes, it was always about conveying a message, or speaking up for something.

Art, to me, is expression, and I expressed whatever resided in me. One of my selected artworks is "On a Diet." This was a painting where a female skeleton is sitting for a meal. The concept behind it was how some young women in the UAE are affected by the desire to lose weight, and suffer eating disorders. I wanted to raise awareness regarding it.

I believe regardless of how many paintings I create, or art I demonstrate, all of them are fueled by the passion to contribute in one way or the other.

I progressed in my career through the art of expression, some of which made headlines, such as, "Mummy and I." It reflects a mother, covered in a black *Abaya* and scarf while clutching her infant. This painting was a general point of view based on the real stories of mothers during UAE's independence in 1971.

As I gained momentum, I participated in a custom toys exhibition at the Dubai International Financial Centre in 2010. I was one of the 100 artists who added individual touches to a 10 cm-high white statue.

I chose the tradition *yowla* dance, and depicted it through a skeleton wearing a *ghutra* and headphones.

I was constantly grooming, and being encouraged to continue my artwork. Each time, I had new ideas, and my creativity including my interest in portraying events, experiences and causes became my signature style.

Soon enough, I was receiving invitations to contribute or

collaborate. In 2011, I received a call from the Dubai Culture & Arts Authority to contribute a mixed-media installation to the Sikka Art Fair, an annual event that commissions and showcases emerging artists based in United Arab Emirates.

I contributed in the 2012 Maritime UAE exhibition which was held alongside the National Day celebrations. The reason behind it was to pay tribute and acknowledge the maritime influence on Emirate culture. My artwork consisted of fish skeletons.

The Dara Chronicles

In 2013, I presented my third solo show, the series named The Dara Chronicles at the Ara Gallery in downtown Dubai. It was different than the usual ones, as it consisted of underwater paintings, mixed-media and digital prints which used X-rays and vintage suitcases.

The Dara Chronicles was based on the brutal and heart-breaking incident of MV Dara, a 120-metre (390 ft.), four-decked vessel, that suffered an explosion and sank on 8th April in 1961, causing the death of 238 people.

The event was truly a havoc. MV Dara mostly carried expatriate passengers from the Arabian Gulf to the Indian Subcontinent.

It should have been just another day when the incident took place. MV Dara had arrived at Dubai on 7th April, and was in the middle of unloading a cargo, and several passengers were getting off or embarking when the wind caught them off guard. According to the Beaufort scale, the wind had surpassed force seven, leading work to completely halt. While this was enough chaotic situation, Dara was hit by another boat, the anchor of which had been dragged in the bad weather. This led the captain to an instant decision, which was to take Dara out of the harbor and surpass the storm. However, fate was at its most unfortunate moment, and Dara experienced a massive explosion, let alone survive the storm.

The passengers, including several officers, crew members and even those who had no intentions of traveling became the victims of an incident they barely saw coming.

The staff managed to put down a life-boat and save some of the passengers but unfortunately, it flipped over due to overload.

From several people losing their lives, to the survivors who wouldn't ever overcome the trauma, many stories were yet to be brought in the light, and I felt as if it was upon me to contribute as much as I could.

Hence, the exhibition began with a footage of me diving underwater, trying to balance myself due to strong currents to create one of my underwater paintings using waterproof, heat proof and against UV light material; the time when I almost drowned as mentioned previously.

I covered several real stories of the survivors, and even of those who had drowned. I realized the information covered by the British media was just the tip of an ice-berg.

Clearly, many of the survivors' suffering was yet to be acknowledged and addressed. I researched, collected data and presented the stories alongside my art work for the audience to know how much more was there to the MV Dara's incident. In November 2014, I took part in an exhibition called Promesse where I was one of the 16 artists who had to interpret Baume et Mercier timepieces.

The year 2014 was quite a career-blooming one for me. This was the year my digital artwork, "Money Doesn't Float," part of the Dara Chronicles was put on auction in London.

By the looks of what I create, the most prominent element is often highlighted as the skeleton. However, if you look closely, it represents inner beauty and focuses more on the bright side.

Most of my buyers are either diplomats or belong to a royal family; mainly because my art got added in many art collections and one of them was, "A Burgeonin Collection."

To acknowledge my passion and individual ingenuity, as well as the creativity of my work, the Shangyuan Art Museum in Beijing arranged a solo exhibition. Several of my artworks were chosen for the gallery's private collection.

I got a diving license, which enabled me to make paintings underwater and made me the first Emirati to do so. I, being an adventurous painter, was fascinated about shipwreck diving, especially the MV Dara. My artworks, which portray the websites I had explored, are extraordinary because they blend my imagination with the history. As an "Ambassador of Art," I successfully conveyed my understanding of the social and personal implications of my Beijing trip by skillfully incorporating colors and shapes into my digital artwork.

In 2017, I put on my fourth solo exhibit, in the Shangyuan Art Museum in Beijing. Going back in time, I often reminisce how I started and where I am now. My very first solo show was held in the Maraya Art Centre in Sharjah in 2010 and was called "The Bright Side of the Bones." The series reflected upon the underrated potential of skeletons. While the world turns to it to examine age and gender, skeletons can provide us the entire story far beyond it. However, it isn't accessible to the naked eye. I truly believe skeletons carry the person's life.

My second was displayed at the DUCTAC Gallery of Light in Dubai in 2011, where ten paintings reflecting life in the UAE were featured.

No wonder my mother saw it coming, and believed in me quite confidently, I was born into a household where my mother was a fashion designer and my father was a photographer.

To be precise, I began my career in painting in 2008. In 2009, the Emirati Expressions: Art from the Heart of the Emirates exhibition at Gallery One showcased my work, which I had produced in two weeks. Other countries where I had exhibited include the Alliance Francaise de Lagos and International Art Exhibition NordArt 2021 in Büdelsdorf, Germany. Moreover, I have shown my work in a number of places in the United States of America.

The "2nd of December Street" project, created by Brand Dubai, the creative arm of the government of Dubai Media Office jointly with Dubai Municipality, engaged an Emirati group of artists including me to decorate the project with my painting of a wall composed of ancient stamps.

The 3 Phase Signal

Through the use of symbolic sine waves, I presented the story of tolerance and human contact.

Overall, my artwork mostly revolved around creativity from the bones and skulls that depicted Emirati life, culture, and history with a cheerful nature that blended the cruel view of the skeletons, especially in "The Bright Side of The Bones" series,
However, I unleashed the possibilities and created another form of my distinctive art in a surreal way. "THE 3 PHASE SIGNAL" that shows us blank faces in some paintings and where others have been replaced with colorful visual effects. From the perspective of their traditional and religious clothes, I left their personalities with only their distinguishing characteristics, and transformed their human characteristics into empty color fields.

I tried to stress, in line with the colorful and constantly changing visual representation, the importance of deepening the relations between different nationalities and religions. It demonstrated my inherent belief that although our humanity is the cause of all our cultural differences, it was and will always be the strong bond, which binds us always.

I have been a part of more than a hundred exhibitions at various major art institutions and exhibition venues, including the Art Science Museum at Marina Bay Sands, Singapore (2014); Kunstquartier Bethanien, Berlin. Moreover, my work has been shown in numerous galleries, including shows in Dubai, Abu Dhabi, and various European locations.

I wasn't just a hard worker fueled by passion, but was also actively looking for new challenges in my career, participating in artist residency programs around the world, including Art House Düsseldorf's artist residency programme in Germany (2016)

Watching Over You

This digital art series represents the human condition as it has been experienced by most people at some point in their lives due to the ongoing global pandemic, forcing us to isolate, quarantine, or even lock-down. I perpetuated a heritage in symbolism that goes back to poetry and art. For example, a bee represents industry and honey represents sweetness, while the color red symbolizes love. Like the individuals throughout the world who retreated inside their houses, hiding and waiting for the world to go back to its old ways again, the major motifs in my digital artworks printed on uniform, square-shaped plexi glass are placed in a constrained space. In each image, the backdrops are as colorful as the cultural landscapes that exist in each of us. We share this experience with each other as a worldwide community. Above the realistic scenes, the disembodied cat eyes stare at the viewer with a hopeful interest. The stares of these hidden creatures, who are seemingly unable to be seen, reflect the gazes of the onlookers. What is it that you are looking at? Are you in search of a better, more caring, and more conscientious future?

I was constantly thriving, and as time passed, the size of my audience was increasing. This, to me, was an achievement. I often looked back to when I used to be in my first studio, with my friend, the skeleton.

I compared myself with who I used to be, and who I was now. I often thought of whether the "then me" knew I had enough room to become who I was today. I was just a teenager, utilizing my skills on what I loved doing. For me, it was never about making money or getting famous. I was just a mischievous child with a gift. However, along the way, I started to see how what I loved doing, could bring me and even the world more than what it was at that moment. Hence, I took the route less travelled, with no destination, as success does not have an end, it's only about the journey of one milestone to the other.

Chapter Four

Bruised, yet Blooming

"While top and bottom may be two different directions, the only thing common in it is the need to have someone and share it with them…"

While my career was blooming and bright, my personal life was as lonely and dull. It was then when I realized whether it was a struggle, or a celebration, the feelings of having someone to share it with was an achievement on its own.

I was married, and it was purely arranged. They basically called my parents and my parents accepted the guy for me. They weren't really Emirati people. However, we had to part our ways. The decision to part was mutual, and it ended quite peacefully and in good terms. Even though he was nice to me, and he treated me well, but there was something missing.

I felt as if I had rushed into the relationship and the compatibility as a spouse wasn't there. He was always an amazing friend, but I needed someone more like me, and my personality. He was somewhat a completely different person. My art to me was everything, and the least I wanted in my better half was to understand it. He did value it, though. He always supported me in my festivals and museums, and was there to cheer for me.

I admired him, but I longed for someone who spoke the language of my art, and this to me was a priority.

Hence, my marriage ended in six months, 3 of which were about involved in filing for divorce.

This experience for me was enough to understand I wasn't made for an arrange marriage. Instead, I prefer to know someone personally and gradually let things align themselves.

However, in time I came to know it wasn't as easy as I thought it would be.

To find someone I could vibe with was gradually becoming a dream unfulfilled.

My intentions were pure, and I was only looking for a serious life partner; the kind to get married with immediately. I tried everything, from trying several dating apps where one swipes left or right according to their preferences, to meeting out on a coffee with people my friends recommended me. It was then when I realized finding a true companion isn't some junior high problem to be solved.

I was on the road to finding my other half, and apparently, it wasn't quite the road trip I had envisioned it to be.

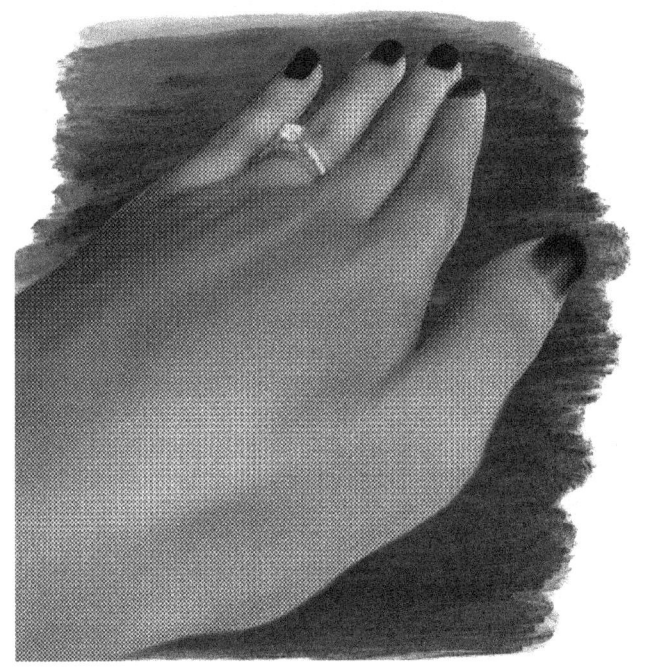

From embarrassing moments to hurtful situations, I was met with all.

In my experience, dating apps are a complete waste of time. They only provide you ground to fool around and pass your time. Since I was looking for something serious, I barely got something worthy out of it. In fact, it only made me more anxious, and question myself on how and why I had come to this point! After a few unworthy interactions, I deleted the application instantly. It was a relief! I was already commented and judged for using applications like these. Apparently, it was hard for people to believe my intentions were purely to settle.

It was gradually consuming me, and I have to admit, I began feeling a bit upset.

All I wanted was a companion, it turned out the world was in search of something much more temporary.

I am an artist, I look beyond everything I see. My feelings generate from the depths of everything I touch, or even come across with.

When I say companion, I didn't just want someone to settle down with, I wanted a connection, a bond quite strong, and someone whom I could celebrate with, and someone who could be there for me in case I fall.

I did not stop. I wasn't the one to back down this easily. Hence, I came across a lady who was a match maker. She said she could find me the exact match for me by asking my requirements.

I have to say, I wondered if she was superficial.

One day she sent me a message and said she found me a guy. She forwarded his picture to me, and I was kind of looking forward to it. She asked if I would allow her to send my pictures to him. Funny because I was on the internet!

I told her to look it up online, and she came back telling me he wasn't interested.

This took the best of me at the moment. I began asking my friends if there was something wrong in my pictures or information. I wasn't sure.

Closure is important. It sets you free.

My friends used to soothe me saying there wasn't anything wrong with me, or my social platforms. However, the thought of someone backing off just because of my presence on the internet didn't fit well with me.

The search was tricky. I came across people who were disguised and underneath their masks were intentions not aligning mine.

I ended up with disappointment so many times that I began questioning whether there was something wrong with me. I truly believed it. I didn't know what it was, but I felt as if there was something missing, or maybe I wasn't what people were looking for those days.

With time, my concern only grew and I ended up scheduling sessions with a therapist. The therapy was to identify what was wrong with me and then work for its solution.

However, it didn't went exactly as I had planned!

My first session was over the phone where the therapist only extracted details about me, my life and how I was feeling. The second session was a video call where I ended up being kicked out. Apparently, the therapist thought I was fooling around and there was nothing wrong with me. When the call hung up, it took me a while to even accept what had happened. I was caught so off guard that I didn't know whether to laugh or be embarrassed. It's a mystery till date. Well… at least I got my answer, apparently, there was nothing wrong with me!

I always fantasized my man as someone active, sporty and adventurous. I wanted my other half to be as challenging as me. Even though him being handsome was part of my imagination as well; not shorter than 180 cm, dark brown eyes, perhaps a lawyer or worked in the military, to be particular, intelligence was what intrigued me the most!

I wanted to have intellectual conversations with deeper meanings. The kind of other half that fulfills your soul, and contributes to the meaning in your life.

However, it took me a while to realize there was nothing wrong with me. Perhaps what I required was just rare.

In time you shall see there was nothing in you to mend, and what is destined for you will eventually end up with you.

It may feel like an uphill fight to love oneself but if loving one is something that comes naturally, why is it so difficult?

I sensed a desire to love myself, and I had an idea of what it meant to value myself too, but the ideas in my head immediately went to negative conclusions.

Once we've gotten used to thinking in a specific manner, it becomes really difficult to go back.

You are not enough!

You do not matter!

These are words you would never say to someone you cared about and loved. Would you say this to your child, your best friend, or your parent if you could communicate like this? However, the voice inside my head, my own internal monologue often said this to me...

When it comes to being critical of oneself, most individuals are downright brutal. They often have little control over it; they simply do what comes naturally. In other words, for some individuals, it is just part of the culture which pushes us to be humble and humble-minded. For others, being critical and demanding may have turned into a motivation tactic, as they hope that being motivated to improve would spur them to work more. However, it wasn't the same for me.

Covid had me stuck; the isolation, the constant number of deaths, and not being able to share the chaos within me was consuming me. I often felt lonely thinking I would never end up with someone.

One of the reasons this occurs is because we frequently build the basis of our views about ourselves based on how we speak to ourselves. We must be very careful with our words since our beliefs are formed on the basis of what we say to ourselves. According to these beliefs, we act and behave, impacting everything around us. I could keep telling myself, for example, "You are not good enough, you are a failure," which would cause me to believe that this is real, and as a result, I could end up performing in a way that confirms this to be true. There are several situations in which a person could refrain from making an attempt at something, believing it is outside their realm of capability.

However, through my triumphs, I observed the only unfortunate event is the fact that you didn't do anything about it. Hence, I decided the least I could do is change my lifestyle. I began making my own healthy meals. I started training and focused on fixing my back posture by strengthening my back muscles.

As we communicate with ourselves, our choice of words has a profound impact on our self-perception.

The desire to be nicer to oneself is frequently met with fear as individuals believe that self-acceptance involves giving up on oneself and accepting things as they are. Although this is not completely accurate, this is not completely inaccurate either. The first step to being nice to ourselves is taking the long view and working towards our long-term goals and ambitions rather than pursuing short-term happiness. It is a nice analogy to see it as if you were a parent.

Would you allow that youngster to let every whim rule their decisions, miss school simply because they didn't feel like attending, and give up on their goals and ambitions because they were tired or bored? Even if you love them, you probably wouldn't want to – because you want what is best for them in the long-term. We should provide ourselves with the kindness and compassion we would show to others, as well as providing ourselves with the support and encouragement we would show to others. In other words, it involves considering our best interests both in the long-term and the short-term.

Listen to your subconscious self. What does it have to say? How does it make you feel? Kindness to yourself may help you alter every aspect of your life since you now have the support and backing of the person who can help you reach where you want to be and achieve your aspirations.

When you enjoy your work and those with whom you do it, you are irreplaceable.

You have a big impact on other people's lives when you are thoughtful, generous, and considerate of others.

You make a difference when you leave the world better than you found it.

As you raise the standard on your work as you go about doing it, you have an impact.

When you teach, forgive, and continuously educate, you have an impact.

When you do things to show that you care about the people in your life, you are making a real difference.

When children want to be like you, you are important.

By refusing to recognize the world as it is, but insisting on creating a better version of it, you count.

When you enter into a room, it brightens because you matter.

Hence, it took me a while to grasp the value of my own self, but I ultimately was out of the darkness. It was evident. I mattered, and

I will eventually end up with someone who believes the same.

When you love yourself, you tell the world you're lovable and eventually come across someone who does.

As soon as I understood this, I knew I could bloom with the bruises. In fact, the very reason I could bloom were the bruises. They were the reminders of my strength, and how I overcame every obstacle in my way, not just with willpower, but positivity as well.

***

I despise wearing watches and only do so on rare occasions. I do not even wear gold or diamonds. Most of my clothing consists of a plain black T-shirt, jeans, and a pair of athletic shoes for me to be considered stylish. Others wonder if I'm wearing the same thing as I did yesterday because much of it is identical. This allows me to wake up without worrying over what to wear and how to match it with other things. As long as people are talking about me, I don't mind!

Who doesn't enjoy being in the spotlight? I am not really the one to take hours and get ready, observing all the details on my face to hide them, or enhance my features. I have always believed in minimalism and low maintenance.

We all have moments in our life where we want to give up on our various endeavours. Occasionally, we give up before we've even gotten off the ground. We also tend to quit just as we are about to achieve a significant breakthrough, which is essential.

However, we must keep in mind that life's most trying experiences frequently lead to its most memorable ones. We should live by the slogan "Keep going." In the end, difficult circumstances produce resilient individuals. If anything, we should be afraid of not trying enough.

Anything is achievable in the world of fantasy. You have the option to keep trying till you succeed as long as you are still alive, well, and free. But, of course, you must be practical while setting goals.

In no way should the phrases "give up" and "give up on anything" be used interchangeably. The word "no" in particular should not be part of your dictionary even. One of the most enthusiastic and powerful creatures ever to walk this world is you, me and each human being.

If you're like most people, you have no idea how many positive attributes you possess. And when you're feeling down, a brief reminder of your potential may dramatically lift your spirits. To experience success, you must first endure temporary failure. Keep this in mind at all times.

Those who quit up after a setback will fail, but those who keep trying will achieve success.

You get to make the decision! Risk-taking is a need if you want to do anything unprecedented. You'll have challenges along the way, but staying focused on your objective will get you through them. Instead of moaning about the things you lack, take action to acquire them. Put everything else on hold and concentrate only on achieving your objective. Giving up is not an option if you want to achieve your objective. It's a sign that you've come to terms with your failure. Don't let fear of failure stop you from achieving your goals.

Problems are a part of everyone's life. It's a component of life that's always been there and always will be. Even successful individuals have to go through hard times before they can taste success for the first time. In order to be successful in life, you must learn the art of dealing with disagreements, conflicts, and rejections.

Whenever you feel like giving up, ask yourself: Is giving up a solution to my problems? This will help you stay focused. If that's the case, carry on with your task. Consider all the individuals you'd be able to please if you were a success. Spend some time alone with yourself to recharge your batteries. Consider the kind of life you want to have after you succeed in your objective.

Imagine that you are already recognized and rewarded for your accomplishments at a university, a college, or on a television show.

Don't give a damn about the folks who don't like you. Your haters are the very first people who see potential in you. Consider this the reason to keep going.

Even if you put forth a lot of effort, you may not see any results. It's possible you may give up. However, keep in mind that if achieving success was simple, then everyone in the world would have done so. Don't be afraid to follow your aspirations. Good times become wonderful times if you have hope, and difficulties are solved as well. The sky's the limit. Avoid being deterred from pursuing your goals by someone who has given up on them.

Whether we are defeated or conquered is always a choice we make. Every individual on this world has the inner power and capacity to do incredible things. Even if we don't get the win right away, as long as we keep going, everything is possible.

There are no exceptions in our world; everyone is born vulnerable and weak. We all gain new values, beliefs, and personal convictions over time, and those things create the basis on which we build our life. You must believe in yourself and think that you are deserving of success as well as a pleasant and comfortable life.

You must have the conviction that you will succeed and leave a lasting impression on the next generation. Nothing in the world - not even yourself - can stop you now. The only way to achieve your goals is to maintain believing in yourself and pursuing your ambitions no matter what.

Even though you're going through a hard patch right now, remember that nothing in life is guaranteed to stay the same. Most things have the potential to, and will, change throughout time. If you hold on and keep trying, eventually the problem will go away on its own. Imagine drilling a water well in an area known for its rich supply of underground water.

However, despite excavating to a depth of 50 meters, they come to the incorrect conclusion that water does not exist. A second person arrives the next day and digs 1 meter deeper, where they discover plenty of water. If you're serious about succeeding in life, you must be persistent.

There is nothing else that compares to the sense of achievement you will have when you finally achieve your goals. When you eventually achieve after years of work, the satisfaction of having done well makes up for the years of hardship.

When a mother hears her new baby's first cry, it's as if the months of anguish and discomfort have vanished, and all that's left is taking care of this tiny human being.

Because we have life, we have the ability to have hope and limitless possibilities.

Nothing will be difficult for a person who believes in the power of positive thinking. Throughout history, millions of people have demonstrated this. Only on the day of your death will you be devoid of all possibility.

Chapter Five

The Ripening

As time passes by, you begin to understand the very things that once bothered you. You look at life, and realize you see right through it, and that's when you know the bruises were worth it...

Is LIFE easy for you? Is it simple, or is it more difficult than that? Boring, stagnant, or lacking in novelty are all terms that describe simple life. Simplicity, on the other hand, is sometimes just as attractive.

Even though life is straightforward, we have a tendency to overcomplicate things. If you'd asked me about this earlier, I'd have said that those who claim it's straightforward are liars because how can life be anything but a jumble, a source of worry and complications? That's no longer my response.

Humans, not life, are the most difficult to understand. Our tendency is to overthink it all and turn a hill into a mountain. We want others to understand our needs without having to express them, as if they had telepathic abilities. We are the ones that, when trying on a dress, question whether or not it will be liked by everyone. The ones that weigh the calories and exercises they'll have to do the next day before indulging in any comfort food. We are the ones that are constantly looking for nuances. And then there are those of us who claim that life is difficult. Even while all of this fakery can be distracting, there are times when we desire for a simpler time.

Let's face it, no one likes a complicated life, and if given the choice, most people would choose a simple one over anything else. So, what can you do to simplify your life instead of wishing you had someone else's easygoing lifestyle?

Eliminating non-essentials from your life isn't difficult, but it can have a significant impact. Little behaviors that you don't even realise you have can have a big impact on your life. Take a look at your routines for a second and make a start with those.

That delicious burger is calling your name, so go ahead and dig it. The exercises and calorie counting can wait! Alternatively, if the dress across the street appeals to you, go ahead and purchase it! Who cares if the rest of the world doesn't like it? Everything is fine as long as you do.

Stop worrying about what other people may say and start dancing in the rain if you want to. You'll never see those people again.

Overanalyzing is the root of half of life's troubles, according to research. The tendency to overthink might contribute to mental health issues. Make the following changes and you'll see improvements in your mental health and overall well-being.

When I'm feeling down, I'll sit on my balcony and look up at the stars for a while... It's amazing how small your issues seem when you stare up at that limitless night sky filled with millions of stars. To realise that a simple existence has always been right in front of you, but that you were merely oblivious to its true beauty because of your preoccupation with trivial matters

The lives of no one are ideal or flawless. Everyone on the planet has their own set of issues to contend with. So, instead of wallowing in self-pity about what you can't do or attributes you lack, focus on being grateful for what you do have. Our minds are incredibly potent, and whether you want to use that power as a curse or a blessing is entirely up to you. When you're aware of the beauty in the world, life gets lovelier; nevertheless, when you're solely aware of the problems, it becomes more complicated.

Just like in a mirror, everything in life is a reflection of your true self.

So, instead of stressing, try to laugh a lot, live fully, and love deeply.

I always felt that the more popular I got, the less my social circle became. The friends I have, or the people I hang out with, they keep changing. At the beginning, I had several friends but through time I felt they weren't as focused in their career as I am, and that kind of ticked me off.

Through time, I realized I lost a lot of friends. I must admit, it does feel sad at times, but was it really my loss? You aren't supposed to lose friends. Friends stick together till the end.

But yes, as my circle kept changing, being emotionally attached to someone wasn't really an option.

What's the point of pouring your heart out to someone who's not here to stay?

So yes, I'll stick to what I initially believed…

You do not lose friends.

My routine now is just work, or spending time with Khulood, my younger sister. Khulood is a graphic designer and works on animation. Hence, we have this art understanding and language that helps us bond well. Besides, as I said earlier, she's the only person who knows how to make me giggle and laugh. Weekends for me are for work as well. Mainly because work is my life, my passion and my purpose.

I always had a knack for gaining knowledge and exposure, not just in my field but regarding everything. In my spare time, I often read law books, just to know more about things.

I want to be able to have conservations with people from different aspects of life. Hence, I always indulge in things quite far from my field. I once even took classes by a pilot, just to gain knowledge, and be able to talk about it.

As far as my social media platforms are concerned, I am more into organic traffic than to run social media campaigns frequently. Although I have ran them before, the intent is to just not fall out of the race.

I believe we shouldn't really show how smart we are, the skill is in just calmly listening and observing.

The company I own now, THE PAINTLY STORE, reflects automation, as everything is automated and outsourced. I don't believe having a staff on my company's license. This is because it becomes easier for me to let them go if they do not align with my goals. In addition, I do not commit to them about anything. Hence, outsourcing work is much better for me. Moreover, I always believed in flexible hours. It's better to work efficiently from your comfort zone, while living a life, than to just be restricted to a single place with committed hours to fulfill.

Everything is integrated with my bank as well, meaning the system I've chosen to work in automatically runs the process instead of asking me to be in a location.

One of my best experiences was creating artwork while traveling around the world on an airline, train, and cruise ship every morning as I looked out the window at a new scenery. Evidently, this is the best benefit of owning and working in an automated work environment. There really are no restrictions!

The most beneficial thing about pursuing this field is that you may travel for free across the world by applying for art residencies that pay your art material costs and provide you free lodging, transportation, and allowance!

***

Before now, I was quite an over thinker. I exaggerated even the littlest of things.

I remember there was a time when someone on the internet altered a semi-naked picture with my face on. Thankfully it was taken down but it really affected me.

What still stays in my mind is the question of why someone felt the need to go out of their way and shame me like that. The intent was specifically to cause me harm. However, it didn't hold me back for long. The authorities I approached took it down and ensured me if it happens again they would apply a severe approach and track the perpetrator down.

Why did I go through something like that? Why did someone even think I deserved it?

I believe it was some guy I rejected, not to forget the number of men I tried to jell in with, it just could be true!

Even though I come off as a happy and positive person, I dealt with severe issues under the table.

Throughout my life, I was always concerned about why my skin was sensitive, and I bruised easily. Moreover, I didn't just bruise easily, it took me quite a while to heal as well.

It was only after 33 years that I found out I have a blood condition; the kind that doesn't let it clot easily.

Despite its richness, Arabic is a language I struggle with. Because

English is my first language and I was reared in the United States, I find it simpler to converse in English. To yet, I've failed miserably at mastering the Emirati accent; but, I strive, and I respect those who criticize me so that I may improve my speech even more. It's even more difficult for me to convey my art in Arabic, but I'm trying and I find absolutely no reason to back down. When giving a presentation to someone who speaks Arabic, I'll ask if I may convert to English instead of Arabic because it's simpler for me. Most people accept this, not realizing it's because English isn't their first language.

***

There are a few things I have learned and would like emerging artists to know ahead of their time. I always want to guide people like me, who consider art their purpose and more than just a money and fame building process.

I want them to have what I didn't at my time, and that is a mentor, a guide and someone who is there to tell you it's going to be alright! Here are a few pointers for you to remember:

1. It's just too expensive to send artwork back and forth when you're involved in so many international art shows. As an alternative, I'd collaborate with the gallery to have my digital

artworks produced there instead, generating more money while lowering your expenditures. To transfer ownership of an artwork, you can use an NFT platform or by signing a digital certificate.

2. In exchange for visibility in the news and on social media, artists might agree to show their works with groups. However, it takes almost two years to get acknowledged as an artist. After that, merely stop them from abusing you by sending you such requests on a regular basis. Ask for a fee, such as an hourly rate, insurance for your artwork, travel expenses, or even housing costs, in exchange for your services. Remember! If you maintain your composure, people will respect you more.

3. Be upfront and honest with the gallery members who are representing you, and if you have any concerns, let them know. You have no idea how quickly things will return back to normal for you.

4. Never go out looking for art collectors or buyers; simply

make excellent art and they will come to you. And I assure you, they most definitely will!

5. Promote your artwork on social media to get more sales, according to my observations. Just make sure your social media adverts are aimed at the correct demographic. The key is in the algorithms! However, it isn't necessary for you to learn and implement all the analytics. If you want assistance with social media, you may turn to social media agencies.

Just know that everyone has their time, and you're worthy of everything regardless of what people think. We believe we need validation and appreciation from others, while in reality, the first person we need anything from is us.

You are your very first fan.

Has starting something new in your life ever made you nervous? For example, if you don't complete a task on time, you'll get really anxious. Until you have lost all optimistic thinking and are afraid to begin anything new. Maybe now is the moment to not underestimate yourself because if you do that all the time, you will never grow up and go on to the next stage in your life.

In order to not underestimate yourself, you must ensure the following pointers are catered:

1. Accept the fact that failures are a part of life. Even the most successful people have failed several times before finally succeeding. We learn from our mistakes and make better decisions the following time around because of them.

2. Refrain from comparing yourself to others; remember that you are an individual with your own set of skills and abilities. Because of this, comparing oneself to others is a waste of time and energy.

3. You won't know what you are capable of unless you are forced

to accomplish anything.

For the most part then, it's because you are afraid of failing in life and being criticized that you feel you underestimate yourself. Without even trying, you've already surrendered defeat without ever having lost a game of life.

Chapter Six

For You

"All you need is someone to remind you that it'll all be alright in the end."

Throughout my life, I've noticed how people judge my life to be the perfect one from afar, but it is otherwise. We all have our storms to deal with, and I no longer wish to have a storm-free life. If I could go back and change anything about it, all I'd do is whisper in my ear to never give up.

We are powerful enough to calm the chaos, all we require is support, motivation; perhaps a little push towards the greater good.

Anxiety may be useful if it motivates you to act and find a solution to a problem. Worry may become an issue if you're always thinking about "what ifs" and "worst-case situations." Doubts and worries that don't go away may be crippling. They can drain your emotional stamina, raise your worry, and cause problems in your day-to-day activities. You can teach your mind to be more relaxed and to see the bright side of things.

Negativity just harms you; it has no beneficial effect on anyone else. It just depletes your emotional reserves and pulls your attention away from the things that are truly essential in life. That drive is being sucked away from something constructive and beneficial, like feeling grateful for the blessings you have in your life right now. Being grateful is being appreciative, counting your blessings, enjoying the little things, and recognizing what you have been given in life.

So, what exactly is a source of worry? The mind prefers to cling to what is already well-established. Predictability appeals to you. You're worried that a sudden change of circumstances may upset your well laid plans. The more you focus on your anxieties, the more worried you will feel.

Every type of anxiety, in truth, stems from an underlying lack of trust. You have lost faith in life's kindness.

In spite of the fact that everything is possible, you tend to assume that things will go wrong rather than well.

So, just for today, resolve to lessen your worry. It all begins with your decision. 'Calm down,' say to yourself when you look in the mirror. Everything will be well in the end. Everything is going to work out perfectly. Just take it easy.' And believe me, if you learn to relax and wait for an answer, your mind will answer the majority of your queries.

There's no need to worry; everything will work out fine.

Really. It'll all work out in the end.

The worst is about to happen, and you blame yourself. It's possible that you're to blame, but that's immaterial. It's critical to keep in mind that your current situation is only temporary, and things will improve for you in the future.

There are people who genuinely love you.

The same people who loved you in the past will continue to adore you now that you've achieved greatness. No matter how much of what's going on is due to you, Remember that you deserve this love. In the meanwhile, take a moment to reflect on all the ways the world is better because you're here. Keep a mental list of every time you've made someone smile, whether it was the guy at the grocery store, or the woman/man you chat with even though you're sleepy. Try to recall all the times you did what was right, what was best, or what was necessary for us. Remember the moments when everything went according to plan and you felt great. Keep in mind the times when everything will fall into place once again.

Let go of the desire to be a better version of yourself or to have done better. Everything you've listed is a non-starter. Wishing to be someone other than who we have become now is to believe the seductive illusion that our errors are a reflection of our flaws and thus unworthy of forgiveness.

Mistakes happen all the time. In other cases, these things are merely unfortunate circumstances that we had no control over. Unpleasant things are happening.

That pain in your chest isn't your fault, and you don't deserve it either.

It's not uncommon for decent people to suffer at the hands of evil ones. Think of it as a way to improve your ability to love yourself.

Pay attention to the positive aspects of other people, especially the people you care about. Tell them how much you appreciate the characteristics they possess that help you cope with your pain. It is nice to express gratitude to others for their unique qualities.

There will be no problems.

Make an effort to accept this and hang on to the sense of relief that comes with letting go of the past.

Allow yourself to totally let go.

Keep in mind that everything in life is a blip on the radar, and this task is no exception.

It's possible that you're going through something that's more than just a passing phase. It may appear as though the entire system is about to come to a grinding halt. You're either going to lose something important soon, or you've already lost it.

The best thing about this existence is that nothing is ever truly lost in it. Though we must say our goodbyes, the things and people we have left behind live on in our memories and in deeds and kindnesses that this catastrophe cannot undo

You'll look back on today and be amazed by your character's strength and your confidence in the future when it doesn't hurt as much anymore. You won't be the only one who is taken aback, but you won't realise it. That's something I'm well aware of, and I can assure you it's accurate.

It's all going to work out just great. Believe me.

Try to picture it in your mind's eye by closing your eyes. If you're unable to see it, imagine a time when everything is perfect. Even if this isn't feasible, take joy in the little things like seeing children giggle at the playground, winning a raffle, or having the entire row to oneself on a late-night trip. Make an effort to include yourself in the list of lovely things.

You'll be OK, I promise you that.

For whatever reason, your day may be a complete flop. You may be seen as the biggest fool right now. You may feel as if everything you've worked for has been thrown away, and you're left with nothing.

Sometimes life is cruel, but that's just part of the experience. The severity is simple to overlook while observing from afar, but when you're in the middle of things, it can seem overpowering no matter how hard you try to ignore the harshness. Everyone will assure you that everything will be alright in the end.

Right now, you have to experience your world being flipped upside down, causing your ideas and ambitions to be challenged and maybe altered forever.

In those moments of self-doubt, you begin to examine alternative realities, discover bravery you weren't aware you possessed, and alter your views that haven't served you well in the past.

Rejection stings, but failure stings much more than rejection. It's during times like this that we question whether or not everything will be alright in the end.

Is there any chance you're going to get out of this mess?

The answer is obviously yes. Nothing you've been through will last indefinitely. Today is only a blip on the timeline of your existence. When it comes to seasons in life, some provide all the fruits and joys you could hope for, while others are harsh, cold, and shrouded in clouds that distort your view of the world.

Today may be a cyclone in your life, but there will be a lull at some point in the storm.

Even if you're not OK, it's alright to not be fine.

It's difficult to accept the fact that things aren't perfect. If you let your mind, it will tell you all kinds of falsehoods like "you're not good enough" or "you'll never have a regular life again."

The lies you tell yourself are only explanations for where you find yourself right now. When you lose the mental fight, these falsehoods become facts.

No one, not even myself, is a daily winner.

When we lose our jobs, get life-threatening diagnoses, or lose a loved one, or face our own death, we all have days like that. Whipping out your phone every few minutes in the hope that the solution to all your issues would appear in front of you as if by magic is not very useful.

You'll naturally want to check your most-used social networking app while your phone is in your grasp on a particularly difficult day.

You'll watch a highlight reel of everyone's lives around you at that point, which will make you feel even more depressed.

I assure you that everything will be OK again.

I have always had some rules when it came to achieving success. I was never the one to believe it could be handed out just as a reward for hard work. There is quite more to it honestly. I am where I am today due to the determination and the consistency of it. It is more because of the way I managed it all because I, too, am no different than you, and I had storms to deal with as well. Some of the many essential key points to success in my life are:

Consistency is Essential

The message that fresh and different is the way to go...the route to success is all over the place, whether you're on social media, reading a business magazine, or watching TV. These days, the buzzword is "innovation." A new diet craze appears almost every day, with friends hopping on board to be trendy, businesses flipping the industry on its head with a new approach, and everything in between. It's all about being different and distinctive. What happened to the old-fashioned virtue of constancy? While it may seem counterintuitive, being consistent is generally preferable. Many people underestimate and undervalue consistency as a life strategy, yet it has served many individuals well and may serve you as well.

What does it mean to be consistent, exactly? Start with what it isn't, and then go on to what it is. Keeping a consistent attitude does not imply giving in or settling for anything that doesn't benefit you in any way (personally, professionally, or otherwise). It doesn't imply you to adhere to archaic customs or ideas that don't hold water in today's society. Let's face it, things are changing at a rate that has never been seen before. Consistency does not imply being the same all the time.

So, what does it entail to be a reliable source? To be consistent, one must perform what has proven successful in the past. It implies relying on what has worked before. Simply because the latest relationship expert/business tycoon/fitness guru says so doesn't mean you should change what's working.

To be consistent, one must be regular and constant in their behavior. To see results, you must work consistently. All aspects of life, from job to home to social activities, are affected by this. Working exercise three times a week regularly is far preferable to working out vigorously every day and eventually exhausting yourself. You must put in the work if you expect to see results. There's no avoiding it now.

What steps can you take to make your life more consistent? Let's say you're trying to lose some weight. To yo-yo die or to constantly eat properly with occasional snacks here and there in moderation, which leads to slower but more stable and lasting weight reduction, which do you believe is preferable? Consider starting your own firm, but don't follow the example of the latest Silicon Valley startup and try some new viral sensation of a plan.

What happens if you stick to your guns but nothing goes your way? Give everything some time to settle down. Patience is required if you want to see the forest for the trees. Take a step back and consider the larger picture in a few months. Consider whether or not you were steadfast throughout. A solid foundation is created by following a well-defined strategy consistently and steadily.

So, why don't we hear more about those who have found success via hard work and dedication? It's boring since it's not enticing or appealing in any way. As a culture, we've learned to appreciate the uncommon, eccentric, or wacky that makes something special. Those success stories are great, but they represent a very small portion of all triumphs. What's more? In spite of this, those companies would not be where they are now without a certain level of constancy.

As a result, strive for uniformity in all of your endeavours. It's a win-win situation. Success comes from getting results.

Being Organized

Being Organized Has a Lot of Advantages.

Getting organized is difficult since it requires finding the motivation to put in the effort.

There's no getting around the reality that living in a condition of chronic disorder and clutter produces stress. As you sift through a jumbled space, you may feel overwhelmed. There's the aggravation of always having to look for misplaced belongings. Not to mention the anxiety that comes with being late or unprepared for activities at work, school, or in your social life.

You'll feel lighter and more in charge of your life once you start clearing clutter and putting organizing procedures in place. Finally, you'll have the tranquility you've been looking for.

And what could be a more effective motivator?

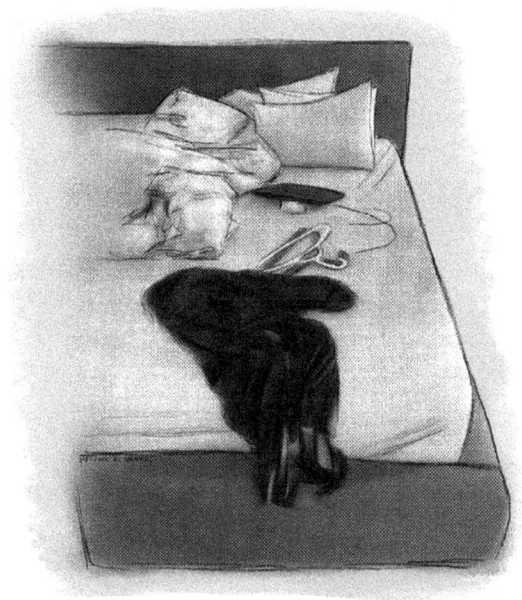

When you get organized, finding what you're seeking for becomes much easier. To-Do lists get done faster, and you're more likely to be on time for important appointments.

Because of this, you're more productive and get more done. And with time, that inner voice starts to change its melody.

Your inner voice will start shouting "I've Got This" instead of the negative messages you've been hearing (such "Why can't I get anything done?"). You'll have a positive self-image and a positive outlook on the future.

Your self-esteem will surge as a result.

Being well-organized increases your output.

You may do more in less time by using basic organizational systems and procedures. To give you an example, when you finally find some time to pay your bills, having an organized bill payment kit saves you from spending time searching for things like a calculator, stamps, and a chequebook.

Similarly, adopting a meal-planning routine decreases the amount of time spent each day trying to figure out what to cook.

More efficient working conditions apply to the workplace as well. You may instantly locate any document you want with the help of a well-organized computer desktop. Distractions can also be reduced by building a system for managing incoming email.

See how it all comes together?

Keeping your affairs in order helps you save money. How?

Here are a couple methods to go about it:

Having a well-organized house means you won't have to buy duplicates of things because you can't find what you already have. You eat out less because you have a decluttered kitchen and a meal-planning habit in place and can prepare meals more easily.
You may earn money by being well-organized.

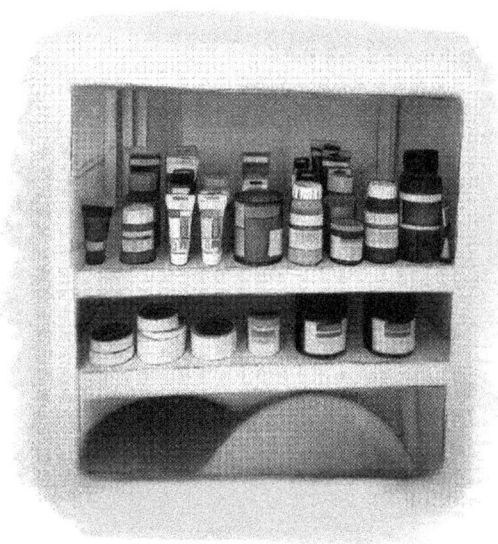

- You may make a lot of money by selling the things you've accumulated throughout your decluttering sessions.

- Refundable purchases may be found with ease if you have the receipts handy.
- More billable hours are generated as a result of increased productivity at work.

When you get rid of clutter, organize your space, and reduce the amount of stuff you have around you, something wonderful happens.

You become more focused and have an increase in physical and mental energy, which allows your creative spark to flare. There are several places where this might happen: In your craft area, kitchen, or studio.

In order to be organized, one must be ready at the time when inspiration hits. Create the circumstances for creativity to flourish so that when you go into creative mode, your physical world is ready to assist you.

Unexpected events may happen to anybody, and when your life isn't utterly disorganized, you're better prepared to deal with them.

When life throws you a curveball, having a well-organized house with established habits and processes allows you to rapidly pivot. Once you've set up the basic processes, you may delegate control to someone else (a spouse, a neighbour, or a co-worker) to keep the household (or workplace) running while you're away.

So, how does it all work in practice?

You'll have more time for self-care when you're more productive. When you're not wasting an hour a day looking for your keys, you can concentrate on eating well and exercising.

Aside from the numerous advantages I've already stated, improved health is a consequence. Since high stress levels are linked to a wide range of health problems, it stands to reason that getting your life under control would make you happier and healthier.

You'll also eat out less since you'll be planning your meals and doing more of the cooking at home, which is a given.

Having a plan makes us better role models for others.

After it comes to raising successful individuals, we as parents have a responsibility to teach our children the life lessons that will help them when they leave the nest. Organizing is, in my humble view, a critical life skill that we should impart to our children.

Having a plan makes it possible for us to assist others.

We may bless others by giving the things we no longer need when we periodically tidy our houses.

While purging the things that are no longer serving us, we have the chance to serve others by donating unwanted home products or building supplies to non-profit organizations in our community.

It's a win-win situation all around! Having a well-ordered life enhances our interpersonal relationships.

The most significant factor is left until last!

Better connections are a major advantage of being well-organized, in my opinion.

Being Punctual is an Important Virtue

Punctuality's value may not apply uniformly across cultures. Life moves at a different pace in different places, someplace meeting times are designed to be ambiguous. There is no doubt that being punctual is important to a man who lives in a culture where being on time is strictly defined, just as a well-rounded man in the West aspires to competence in things like shaking hands, wearing a tie and working out with a kettlebell, even if these things are not practised globally.

This is the reason why.

The Importance of Being on Time

Being on time builds your character and demonstrates your morality. Telling someone you'll meet them at a specific time means you've basically promised to do so. The same goes for being on time and then arriving 15 minutes late. This amounts to breaking your word. A man of his word is a person who is on time.

Being on time demonstrates your dependability. Being on time shows that you are dependable. A person is always at his job, doing the things that need to be done at the moment. Such a person is well-known for their dependability. If they say they'll be there, they will. You can't rely on other people if you're not on time - People around you will begin to distrust your ability to manage time, which will inevitably lead to the question: "If you don't care about time, what do you really care about?"

Being on time increases your self-esteem. When you arrive on time, it shows others that you are reliable and that you can count on yourself as well. More and more promises you keep, the more confident you'll feel. More self-mastery means less reliance on compulsions and habits, which means you'll feel more in control of your life as a result.

Being on time ensures that you are performing at your peak potential. The excitement and tension from speeding, shouting at red lights, and riding someone's bumper make it difficult to concentrate on giving a presentation at work or enticing a date when you're shaking and tired. However, if you arrive on time, or even a bit early, you will have some time to gather your thoughts, go over your notes, and put on your game face.

Being on time strengthens your discipline while also revealing your character. Punctuality demonstrates that a person can plan ahead, pay attention to details, and put pleasure aside in order to accomplish a task.

There is considerable dignity in being expected, according to one who was used to it and who didn't have anything for which he could be wasteful unless it was a lack of promptness.

Being on time demonstrates your modesty. In other words, tardiness and an overestimation of one's value often go hand in hand. When you arrive, people will be happy to see you, but they will be happier if you arrive earlier than expected.

Being on time demonstrates your courtesy and consideration for others. It's a selfish act to be habitually late, because it prioritises your own interests over the interests of others. It would be nice if you had an additional minute to accomplish what you want, but getting that minute at the expense of another is why....

Making excuses for not being on time is a sort of theft. That's a sobering reality, but a reality all the same. You steal precious minutes from others by making them wait for you. Time that may have been converted to cash or employed for personal priorities. They may have made sacrifices to meet you at the agreed-upon time, such as waking up early, cutting their exercise short, or telling their child they couldn't read a story together. Your being late undoes their efforts. Taking 10 dollars from someone else's wallet is a no-no, and the same goes for stealing ten minutes from someone else. To be on time demonstrates that you respect your own time and, as a result, would never consider depriving others of this valuable, yet finite, resource

Being persistently late ruins other people's experiences. Your being late not only wastes other people's time, but it also diminishes the quality of their experiences.

Being persistently late damages your reputation. Delaying meetings with others gives them the impression that you don't respect their time, or that your commitments were more essential than theirs. This makes them feel unappreciated and undervalued. Your out-of-town guest feels alone at the airport, your date feels uneasy at the restaurant by herself, and your child feels abandoned as she waits for you to come with her teacher, all the other children having already been picked up from school.

Not being on time might damage your professional reputation. Whether you work for a company or are self-employed, being late can be detrimental to your career. Many businesses have tight standards about being on time — if you receive a few citations, you're out. Arriving late for a job interview will almost certainly result in your rejection. In the same way that promising to provide something by a given date and failing to do so may cause him to go elsewhere for your services, arriving ten minutes late won't help you win over a new client.

You pay a price for being late. Trying to be one step ahead of everyone damages you in every aspect of your life. Missing a key section of a lecture, an aircraft, a meeting, a wedding, etc. are all examples of missed chances as a result. Driving under the influence causes tension, which can result in accidents and traffic violations. It causes humiliation and makes you come up with reasons why you're late, which puts pressure on your integrity and honesty. On the whole, it complicates your life; practising timeliness is an important step for guys looking to simplify their lives.

The Hunger to Continually Grow and Learn

Since the dawn of time, education has been essential to human survival. Whether it's through official or informal schooling, people are insatiable learners who are always looking for new ways to accomplish things and ways to live their lives.

We continue to learn in some capacity, whether directly or indirectly, from the time we are born until we die. From the moment of birth, through growing up and interacting with our parents and the people in our immediate surroundings to going to school, interacting with peers, and eventually having to learn about the changing generation from their grandchildren, humans have developed a constant desire to learn.

After a certain point in life, people must decide how much they want to strive for; some choose mediocrity, while others aim for the stars by being the most knowledgeable person on earth.

Back in the day, education and learning were more about exchanging knowledge about a culture or a way of life. Children were taught values, customs, and rituals as a method to mould their behavior to fit in with society's expectations.

The child's entire community served as their school, while the elders served as their professors. Learning systems were increasingly institutionalized as civilizations evolved and people were educated outside of their own cultural contexts.

Educational Aspects

When it comes to learning information and becoming an expert, formal schooling can help a kid get there faster. However, in order to become a fully grown and educated adult, one also has to learn the lessons of everyday life and morality along the road.

Lessons in moral science are now part of the curricula of many educational institutions. Empathy, managing feelings, self-awareness, and other traits like communication, problem-solving, judgement, and reasoning would all be developed as a result, providing what is required to successfully navigate life's stages.

An insatiable need for knowledge

Having a burning desire to study is something that we may acquire mostly on their own will. If you're passionate about something, you're more likely to achieve success. Moving mountains, inspiring ideas, initiating projects, and being on the move are all examples of how powerful it can be.

Curiosity drives pupils to solve difficulties, overcome hardships, and achieve their goals. The thrill of amassing information may make studying a pleasurable and fruitful experience.

Incorporating unique approaches and exploring other perspectives makes the previously boring subject a desired one by finding newer ways of studying and executing it in different ways.

The Benefits of Being a Well-Educated Individual

Knowledge is commonly claimed as power. Look for the educated populace in your area and you'll see how effectively they handle life's challenges and deal with them head-on.

Simply being receptive to new knowledge and willing to accept it may do wonders for your brain and intellect.

Today's youngsters will be tomorrow's citizens. We must thus maintain our thirst for knowledge in order to create a better world and a better future for ourselves and those around us. This motivates you to keep growing.

Isn't It Time for You to Grow Already?

In order to get your appetite back, you need to identify your desires and turn them into objectives. When people fail to achieve their goals, it's for one of two reasons: The first is that they aren't sincere about achieving their goal (in other words, they don't desire it). They lack the self-control to keep at it long enough to succeed.

To make your goals come to life, you'll need more than SMART objectives; you'll need a compelling "why" to keep you motivated. Motivating yourself intrinsically is what keeps you striving for more. It comes from having a strong drive and a strong appetite for achievement. If failure to achieve your objective has no repercussions, you're unlikely to succeed. You'll do it if you're able to do without a consequence.

Your reasons will serve as a better source of motivation than the objective itself. Making a daily habit of writing down your objectives and the reasons you want to achieve them can increase your desire to succeed.

The distance between where you are now and where you want to go is mostly determined by how hungry you are, how eager you are, and how motivated you are. If you lack motivation, devote yourself to anything and let it serve as a source of motivation for you.

Life is too short to eat all the time.

When we're this desperate for food, you can guarantee we'll do everything to obtain it. And if that's the case, why do we accept less when we strive for more in any aspect of our lives, whether it's money, health, or happiness?

Unless we "snack" our way through life, we may never reach that level of appetite for achievement. When you're satisfied in small doses throughout the day, it's difficult to generate a burning desire to take significant action.

Your work is "safe," therefore you never start your own company.

You're with someone who "treats you wonderfully," and as a result, you never meet the person your heart longs to be with.

Given that you're not a hunk like some of your pals, you don't treat your gym visits with the respect they need.

You have a comfortable standard of living, so you don't try to provide more value than is necessary to cover your expenses.

You only need a little of the usual to stave off the hunger pains, so you never look for more.

These are the kinds of hunger pains that make you so enraged you'll do everything to get what you want. Many of history's most accomplished men and women rose to new heights as a result of their hardships.

And yet, despite our small "snacks" of achievement, you remain sedated.

You Can't Achieve Your Goals If Your Health Is Poor.

Here are four reasons why excellent health is critical to your professional, personal, and financial success. Being in excellent health and in a good mood are the most thrilling and invigorating feelings in the world. You're all set to get to work and conquer the world. As a result, you're ready to make an effort toward achievement.

You can't succeed in your personal and professional life if you're sick all the time. When I mention health, you might assume I'm talking about bodily health, which is the absence of sickness or disease. That's not all there is to it. When I say health, I'm referring to your whole well-being on all levels: physical, mental, emotional, and spiritual.

Consider each of them in turn, and why they are so critical to your total well-being.

Good mental and Cognitive health.

Cooking, eating, and working require a healthy mental state for you to be able to do them. You must have a sense of calm. You must be able to think critically and rationally in order to make sound judgments. Good mental health affects how you interact with others and your own relationships.

To achieve and maintain excellent mental health, make sure you're getting enough sleep (at least six hours) and eating the correct foods. When you're an adult, getting less than six hours of sleep a night has been shown to negatively impact your overall performance. It can make you feel anxious, tired, and uneasy all day. As a consequence, you'll be less attentive to problems at home and at work, which will have an impact on your outcomes.

You can be impaired by other factors like alcohol or drug usage and hence have bad relationships or even low productivity. Maintaining good mental health necessitates being able to control your stress levels.

In addition, be certain that whatever thoughts enter your head are ones that will be beneficial to you. Don't listen to or watch any shows on the radio or television that don't help you get well. People have been reported to experience harmful effects from excessively violent television shows or films. Also, set time limits on how much time you spend in front of the TV. This will assist you in concentrating on what is most essential in achieving your objectives.

The state of one's physical health and one's employment.

Well-balanced nutrition boosts your defenses against disease. When you're in good physical shape, you'll have more mental and physical energy. Breakfast, lunch, and dinner are all important parts of your day. Protein, carbs, and vitamins should all be included because they are all necessary for healthy bodily processes.

The first meal of the day should be the heaviest in terms of calories. You've probably always been curious as to why breakfast is called that. Keep in mind that if you sleep for an extended period of time, you will likely wake up feeling ravenous. The fasting part is over now, so let's get started! You'll also require energy to get through the day-to-day chores.

We all get the flu or a cold every now and again. Proper nutrition gives your body the tools it needs to combat disease. It's possible that you'll need to take medication from time to time. Well-balanced diets can speed up the healing process while you're sick.

Another strategy to maintain your physical health is to engage in some form of physical activity. Consuming food on your own may not be sufficient. You must establish a daily regimen to ensure that you engage in some form of physical activity. Going to the gym or taking a stroll can both count as forms of exercise? Doing physical activity will help you maintain a healthy weight. It is possible to get overweight if you do not engage in any physical activity and consume excessive calories or foods that are high in fat. Your job and interactions with others will be impacted as a result. Low self-esteem is common among overweight persons, and this can have a negative impact on how they interact with others.

Emotional well-being and how you deal with problems

Do you panic, doubt yourself constantly, and give up when things become tough? What's your reaction when you're treated unfairly? Do you have strong religious beliefs?

Your business's success is directly related to how you treat your customers. The way you relate to your employer and your coworkers is determined by your emotional well-being as an employee. Emotional equilibrium affects how well you get along with your family members. This will help to avoid confusion at home and at work. Success at work is correlated with satisfying personal connections. How well you get along with other people will be determined by your views.

Emotional maturity is essential for long-term success. You may believe that your feelings are under control. Some people believe that their lack of success in life is due to a lack of money or company capital, unemployment, or even a lack of capacity to establish realistic objectives. All of those things seldom have an impact on your life. In the end, it's all about how you react under pressure.

Never giving up is the key to success in life. You have to be true to your principles. Becoming persistent is a skill that has to be learned. You must be able to put up with the injustice of other people. To be clear, I'm not saying to put up with nonsense from those around you. Always remember to show respect to individuals and their viewpoints on topics.

It goes without saying that you should never allow yourself to be mistreated by others. If avoiding such circumstances is your only option, do it. Watch out for things like these, since they might alter your values and how you operate. Don't let your rage get the better of you.

Do not give up on achieving your goals. Have faith in your own ability. Once you've decided what you want to do, make sure you really do it. Avoid being intimidated or persuaded to give up on your dreams because of someone's snide remarks.

Practice meditation.

To obtain inner peace and freedom from the burdens of the outside world, you must first learn to meditate. Meditating helps you learn to look inside yourself and so find inner peace. It aids in concentrating on who you are as a person.

Harmony in all areas of your life is necessary for your success. The extent to which you achieve your life goals is determined by your state of mind, body, emotions, and spirit. Your success is positively impacted when you look after your health and are considerate of the needs of people around you. Eat well, get some exercise, and keep an eye out for anything that can slow you down.

Remember, if I can do it, anyone can. We're all in the same storm, just sailing different boats.

These 33 years of untold secrets are proof of how life may not turn out exactly as you wished in the beginning, but it most certainly will turn out the best for you. Remember, there's a bit of secret is all of us, and that's completely okay.

References

Chapter One

Maisoon Al Saleh
https://en.wikipedia.org/wiki/Maisoon_Al_Saleh (accessed on July 14th 2021)

Chapter Three

The Diptych
https://en.wikipedia.org/wiki/Diptych (accessed on Sept 13th 2021)

The Dara Chronicles
https://en.wikipedia.org/wiki/Dara (accessed on Sept 14th 2021)
https://www.thenationalnews.com/arts-culture/art/exhibition-explores-the-mysterious-dara-disaster-1.471808 (accessed on Sept 14th 2021)
https://saudigazette.com.sa/article/35818 (accessed on Sept 14th 2021)

Dubai Street Museum
https://branddubai.ae/en/project/dubai-street-museum (accessed on Nov 04' 2021)

2nd December Street to get artistic makeover
https://gulfnews.com/entertainment/arts-culture/2nd-december-street-to-get-artistic-makeover-1.1941633 (accessed on Nov 04' 2021)

A Burgeonin Collection
https://artfacts.net/exhibition/a-burgeonin-collection/949707 (accessed on Sept 15th 2021)

Beijing's Shangyuan Art Museum
http://wam.ae/en/details/1395302615919 (accessed on Sept 15th 2021)

Emirati artist Maisoon Al Saleh represents UAE at Beijing's Shangyuan Art Museum
https://www.aviamost.ae/en/emirati-artist-maisoon-al-saleh-represents-uae-beijing%E2%80%99s-shangyuan-art-museum (accessed on Sept 20. 2021)

Dubai artist exposes her diary in China
https://www.artnewsportal.com/art-news/dubai-artist-exposes-her-diary-in-china (accessed on Sept 20. 2021)

UAE Ambassador of Fine Arts' at Beijing's Shangyuan Art Museum
https://dayofdubai.com/news/maisoon-al-saleh-uae-ambassador-fine-arts-beijings-shangyuan-art-museum (accessed on Sept 20. 2021)

DXB to PEK — Maisoon Al Saleh UAE Female Artist Solo Exhibition
https://www.sohu.com/a/135556239_737771 (accessed on Sept 20. 2021)

The 3 Phase Signal
https://etihadmodernart.com/exhibition/984/ (accessed on Sept 20. 2021)
https://issuu.com/xparda/docs/t3ps_-_a5_catalog (accessed on Sept 20. 2021)

Watching Over You
https://www.instagram.com/p/CMe4xYbHRn/?utm_source=ig_web_copy_link (accessed on Sept 20. 2021)
https://art.kunstmatrix.com/en/artwork/maisoon-al-saleh/watching-over-you-08
https://www.agora-gallery.com/exhibition/Transcending_3_16_2021-Artist-Maisoon_Al_Saleh.aspx (accessed on Sept 20. 2021)
https://www.art-mine.com/collectorscorner/maisoon-al-saleh-interpreting-the-multifaceted-works/ (accessed on Sept 20. 2021).

Chapter Six – For you

10 Reasons why Consistency is important.
https://cabiojinia.com/10-reasons-why-consistency-is-important/ (accessed on 9th Oct'21)

Power of Consistency: 5 Rules
https://www.inc.com/eric-v-holtzclaw/consistency-power-success-rules.html (accessed on 9th Oct'21)

The Importance of Consistency
https://www.uexpress.com/life/harvey-mackay/2016/04/25 (accessed on 9th Oct'21)

5 Surprising Benefits of Being Organized
https://selecthealth.org/blog/2021/01/5-surprising-benefits-of-being-organized (accessed on 9th Oct'21)

Benefits of Keeping Organized At Work
https://www.monster.ca/career-advice/article/benefits-of-keeping-organized-at-work (accessed on 9th Oct'21)

Why Being Organized is Vital: The 10 Key Benefits of Being Organized
https://www.refinedroomsllc.com/10-reasons-to-get-organized/?__cf_chl_captcha_tk__=pmd_fnY4sukDDMzhPGizXrnfd7dKbuw2QJnOZ1Oy0_b2CiY-1635792021-0-gqNtZGzNAxCjcnBszQuI (accessed on 18th Oct'21)

Punctuality, a solid virtue
https://www.thestatesman.com/supplements/punctuality-a-solid-virtue-87214.html (accessed on 18th Oct'21)

A Man Is Punctual: The Importance of Being on Time
https://www.artofmanliness.com/character/etiquette/importance-of-punctuality/ (accessed on 18th Oct'21)

What is the importance of punctuality?
https://www.mvorganizing.org/what-is-the-importance-of-punctuality/(accessed on 18th Oct'21)

7 Reasons Being on Time Matters
https://www.cydcor.com/blog/2017/04/7-reasons-being-on-time-matters/(accessed on 18th Oct'21)

Importance of Being on Time
https://www.makemebetter.net/importance-of-being-on-time/(accessed on 18th Oct'21)

The Hunger for Learning – A Reason for Continual Growth
https://www.beaninspirer.com/hunger-learning-reason-continual-growth/ (accessed on 22nd Oct'21)

A Hunger for Continuous Learning
https://www.td.org/magazines/td-magazine/a-hunger-for-continuous-learning(accessed on 22nd Oct'21)

Essential Leadership Qualities – A Hunger to Learn
https://keepthinkingbig.com/essential-leadership-qualities-hunger-learn/ (accessed on 22nd Oct'21)

Good Health Is Essential To Your Success. Here Are 4 Reasons Why
https://medium.com/@chepkoechann/health-is-essential-to-your-success-here-are-4-reasons-why-868b6bd03896 (accessed on 22nd Oct'21)

Why Your Mental Health Is the Key to Your Success in Business
https://www.entrepreneur.com/article/324721 (accessed on 22nd Oct'21)

Acknowledgments

To my mother, and my sister Khulood, art galleries, museums, and organizations I've worked with whom gave me the opportunity and believed in me, to my high school art teacher and to Arthur as the project manager of my book and all the effort he has placed to get this book out to the public was much appreciated.

About the Author

Emirati artist and businesswoman Maisoon Al Saleh, who was born in 1988, has a practice in Dubai as well as elsewhere in the world. In 2010, she earned a degree in Arts and Design from Zayed University. In the fall of 2010, Al Saleh had participated in around 100 exhibitions in 20 countries so far such as, Emirati Expression at Emirates Palace Abu Dhabi, Art Science Museum at Marina Bay Sands, Singapore, Alliance Francaise de Lagos, and ART NOMADS-MADE IN THE EMIRATES EXHIBITION presented by Etihad Modern Art Gallery in partnership with MOMENTUM and The Sovereign Art Prize at Kunstquartier Bethanien, Berlin. These are just a few of the places where Al Saleh's work has been shown. She has also had work included in numerous exhibitions across the United States.

A conversation about Emirati history is sparked by Al Saleh, who questions how we think about history, memory and how they are represented in the media.

www.maisoonalsaleh.com

www.ingramcontent.com/pod-product-compliance
Lightning Source LLC
Chambersburg PA
CBHW040107120526
44589CB00039B/2768